Mother of 0

poems by

Vanessa Ogle

Finishing Line Press
Georgetown, Kentucky

Mother of 0

Copyright © 2024 by Vanessa Ogle
ISBN 979-8-88838-483-1 First Edition
All rights reserved under International and Pan-American Copyright Conventions. No part of this book may be reproduced in any manner whatsoever without written permission from the publisher, except in the case of brief quotations embodied in critical articles and reviews.

ACKNOWLEDGMENTS

Versions of these poems appeared in the following:

"Mother of 0" appeared in *The Shore Poetry*
"Roll Over" appeared in *October Hill Magazine*
"Swatches" appeared as "The Ducks" in *Adanna Literary Journal*

Publisher: Leah Huete de Maines
Editor: Christen Kincaid
Cover Art: Vanessa Ogle
Author Photo: Ross Barkan
Cover Design: Elizabeth Maines McCleavy

Order online: www.finishinglinepress.com
also available on amazon.com

Author inquiries and mail orders:
Finishing Line Press
PO Box 1626
Georgetown, Kentucky 40324
USA

Contents

Whose Mother 1

Mater, Parens, Genetrix 2

On the Road Near the Pontoon Factory 3

Mother of 0 4

Money 5

Roll Over 6

Waiting for the Moon 7

Home Videos 8

Offering 9

I Have Never Won an Award 10

The Red House on the Palindrome Street 11

Swatches 12

Commute 13

Both Sides 14

North 15

Observations (Loss) 16

Hymn 17

Whose Mother

Glances over her shoulder, ear down to railroad track
    Ready for the vibrations on a defunct line? This Mother
Carries her child like a kitten, neck delicate under fangs.
    Hamsters and dogs eat their young—defect or nervousness?—
Mothers that have to be separated, Mothers choosing one
    Baby over the next. Terminology of nature for humans
When it's warranted, nesting until the baby crowns,
    Blood and amniotic fluid ready to drip. Surely you've heard
A belly button isn't genetic, the outie, the innie,
    Flesh determined by doctor, not a Mother at all.
It's been 13 birthdays without my Mother. No
    Colorful candle wax hardening on frosting, no wishes, saliva.
Oh, she's fine! She just doesn't believe in
    Celebrations or jackets or carrying children, with or without fangs.
But she let me sit cross-legged on the church linoleum bathroom floor
    As I examined her skin tag, thinking it was a face.

Mater, Parens, Genetrix

Remember when they tried

to blame perceived
flaws

on mothers

they called

refrigerators,

like refrigerators

didn't save us all?

On the Road Near the Pontoon Factory

I remember the moment we see them, the deer.
The females together. No antlers, of course.
Nothing to obstruct them. Their tails

exposing, not concealing. Big eyes, long
lean fast bodies   bones upturned like
moths ready to flee. No uneven crown, nothing for the men

to count, categorize so maybe they'll be safe,
not upside-down in the bed
of some truck, blood pooling as flies, feasting, invade.

Mother of 0

If you add real to the Google search for newborn you get dolls,
pink dolls, white dolls, weighted dolls, dolls with bare feet, toes curled inward
so they're always moving something, a twitch even in sleep. And isn't it just like life

that adding in the qualifier of real makes something not real—
false, imitation, our best attempt. I wanted to show him what a baby
would be like, covered in that pale slime I assume is from the vagina.

Movies use docile 8-month-olds or dolls, anything but newborns. My mother
thinks Hollywood hospital scenes should use real babies,
weak-necked and wobbly. She wants cheeks with fingernail scratches. Real life.

She's a literalist who stays awake even when she snores, who remembers her surgery,
saying, I kept tapping my arm to let them know I was awake.
She heard them say she was under.

Every choice always seems like the wrong one. On the bus today, I saw a mother
so patient with her child, the baby thinking every red sign was an apple
and I didn't know which one I'd rather be, the one who knows someone is wrong

or the one who speaks without thought, only instinct.

Money

I catch myself holding money like my mother.
Her hands pulling each side, stretching it taut but gently,
Pressure like starch, the bank bills

Already flat, unwrinkled. While waiting in line
She would let her grip relax, almost bending the bill,
Like she wanted to but couldn't bring herself to fold it.

I hate when my hands do the same, all that effort,
Whether it's a twenty or five.
How she hated getting a desecrated bill, words or stamps or scribbles,

Its journey evident then, less of a means to an end,
Tainted. (Her hands and legs are what I think of first.)
If you tear money, it's not worthless, she'd protest.

She knew where it could be sent. The fulfillment of its
Promise, sent back without tape. Someone else
Would piece it back together.

Roll Over

All I ever wanted was
        you. I wore your clothes, we shared a bed for years.

                You are the child, I am the child.
        Maybe I should call you back.

I am nothing like you.
        (Mostly I am not-nothing like you.)

        Someone says you love me

                in your own way. Your own way is not your own.
      (It is the way I love too sometimes.)

Plants all over your kitchen so we walk
        sideways. So much life

                in your house, leaves competing for sun,
        green fighting

to stay green, does it help
        you breathe

                better? Decaying fruit brings more life,
        flies; you've always

eaten your fruit near-rotten.
                            I am taller.
        I forget when I wasn't.

Waiting for the Moon

The night rises.
Where is my moonlight?
I chose the wrong symbol;
I sleep too early for midnight promises.
(And what are promises but a placebo?)
Branches shake at midnight.
In my dream, our footprints stagger.
There was the poet who saw her mother as the moon.
My family speaks like we are separated by galaxies.
I yell, voice from throat, not stomach.
Do I do things because we are connected or because I want to be?
In truth, I haven't seen the moon for months.

Home Videos

Boy-and-girl equally
curlyheaded, duck hair
they called it,

so they fit right in the day
they played in the cattails, twisting
each one, trying to break it near the root,

comforted by the spongy brown
until they broke one—a snap,
the suddenness of it only shocking to

them—all that work just
to forget until it decays into fluff.
My not-yet mother brings them an apple

to share like everything,
the sweetness dripping, their fingertips
sticky, still unsure, swollen and taut

as a kitten's pads. After, they
run in the overgrown grass
that flicks their shins like whips.

The faster they go the more it hurts,
circling each other, their bodies always
parallel but she's the leader: see.

Offering

I looked
at names
on graves at
Greenwood cemetery,
saving favorites in earnest,
like I would use them for my children.
Aurelia. So many Emmas. As a child, I wanted to die
before I bled, thinking it would ensure Heaven. Oh how
jealous I was of baby graves! Little lambs with chipped ears.
Stillborns who still received names. My mother, when in a pleasant
mood, said H-E-double-hockey-sticks. My body doesn't remember
birth; how I've tried.

I Have Never Won an Award

I say this when the trees are yellow or dead,
window raised enough for me to wave my foot through it,

rain dripping off someone's satellite dish and I think,
I really do have a happy life. But nothing

has hit me harder than the lit-up screen,
sun in our dark room, my mother texting, *I'm proud*

to live in America where Kleenex is cheap...

The Red House on the Palindrome Street

Here the cats wait, backs arched,
green eyes unblinking
beyond the gate.

Here long grass rises
only to collapse back
in the wind, hollow after heat.

There's sun,
brightness where
emptiness grows

like a baby.
Afternoon feels
precarious.

There are no cicadas, only
a car, its gas tank clinking open.
Perfect light.

I was never pretty. I was only young.

Swatches
      (to be read silently)

(i) spend all day looking for houses
and (i) live inside the photos,
me, who has never had a home.
even when (i) make the call, (i) bore myself.
beads of sweat run down my stomach,
can (i) hang up on myself?
(i) am jealous
of the ducks (i) see, so at home
in the air and the water and the grass.
my mom once almost-cried
at the beauty of the male duck,
why do they get everything, she said.
women camouflage
and providers, blending into surroundings
so we aren't eaten. the cattails
have exploded now, mid-may, fluff
expanding outside of the tight
casing, taupe pieces now like feathers
of the duck, or dogs shedding in this heat
as (i) find gray hairs in my plastic cutlery.

Commute

I see myself
in the woman
on the train. Emerald
earrings shake with
every rattle, light
making one translucent,
the angle of her red
curl making the other
dark as leaves.
I don't have my
ears pieced and
I don't arch my
eyebrows like hers,
movement creating
waves that touch
toward her scalp.
Such certainty
she has, thought arched
in consideration
(not disgust), and
I— I am unsure
of most things.
But we sit in a
way that
could make
an almost-X, feet
turned towards each
other until
we both get
off. I don't eat
the banana in
my bag. Instead
I call my mother,
the sweat now cold
from the February
wind. When I get
to the office I
wash my hands with
dish soap.

Both Sides

My mother's family had reunions under the park pavilion,
        gifts wrapped anonymously to be unwrapped with glee,
a good gift hidden in a sea of jokes, money taped
        under Tupperware lids. My cousins and I
spun ourselves sick on the merry-go-round
        at the playground, dizzy walk from tree to tree
with outstretched arms. The roots are raised, pushing up sidewalk.
        I close my eyes and try to hear.
My mother saw her deceased sister in a dream.
        "I'm ok," she said she said. "I'm ok."

A boy once asked me if I had a father.
        After that, I tried to mention him.
I don't know, still, if I say too much or too little.
        The birds haven't woken me in a while. Every time
a boat passes under the bridge, I pause to watch.
        I have picture after picture of ferries and cruise ships.
What could I give to my children? I live in one
        place and think of another. (Who am I, but an extension
of so much pain?) A flower hangs off a fence,
        dangling, downwards. I take a picture of that too.

North

Pine trees blur on the roads that turn to potholes then exit ramps and dirt roads, more pavement, some gravel, past the signs for rest stops, pay-by-the-hour motels, the same five fast food chains, gas station after gas station, prices pennies off. Inside, rows of beef jerky and candy on messy shelves, bathroom doors that aren't locked, tampon dispensers next to the flavored condoms, 75 cents each. By the register, there's a plastic jar marked donations, not tips, a wadded dollar bill swimming in a sea of change. You can each pick out one thing, our mother says, the gum and sunflower seeds and cookies dotting the counter and there'd be an ease in the car, the argument over who gets to sit shotgun forgotten now. The boys will have to pitch the tent in darkness, the same one from last summer and no one can remember if it even had all the poles to begin with, probably not, didn't they lose a piece? If no one sets up this tent then we're not going to the fireworks tomorrow, is the threat, and so the boys figure out a way to make it work, hitting the bright yellow plastic stakes, their feet hammers. Tomorrow we'll go to the beach, swimming, then the arcade, no prizes but for a quarter, bouncy balls, and there's ice cream, too, but I'm not paying for each of you to get an ice cream when we can get a gallon that's cheaper, our mother says. And so we'd stop at the grocery store and get the chocolate-strawberry-vanilla kind and a box of ice cream cones and plastic spoons to scoop that we didn't have to worry about breaking because by the time we got to the car the ice cream was starting to get gooey and we ate it, right there in the parking lot as the rest of the ice cream turned to soup, lid still off in all the excitement.

Observations (Loss)

My juice container says separation is natural…
The billboard on my bus says E V I L…
I was once told I had the best luck…
Streets are naked without scaffolding…
Holiday inventory is three months ahead…
My mother no longer looks the same…

Hymn

she
tells
me
to
be
quiet
like
genes
are
silent—

Vanessa Ogle is a poet and writer. Her work has appeared in the *New York Times*, *The Nation*, and elsewhere. She has worked as a journalist and a photographer, and her photos have appeared in the *Village Voice* and international publications. She served as a Legislative Director and Communications Director in the New York City Council. She received her BA from Stony Brook University and her MFA from Hunter College. In addition to her writing and legislative work, she is an educator.

www.ingramcontent.com/pod-product-compliance
Lightning Source LLC
Chambersburg PA
CBHW022110080426
42734CB00009B/1545